The Geographer's Wife

THE GEOGRAPHER'S WIFE

poems

BART EDELMAN

Red Hen Press | Pasadena, CA

The Geographer's Wife

Book design by Anamaria Ramos

Edelman, Bart, 1951–
The Geographer's Wife: poems / Bart Edelman.—1st ed.
p. cm.
ISBN 978-1-59709-169-5
I. Title.
PS3555.D389G47 2012
811'.54–dc22   2011025193

The Los Angeles County Arts Commission, the National Endowment for the Arts, and the Los Angeles Department of Cultural Affairs partially support Red Hen Press.

First Edition
Published by Red Hen Press
Pasadena, CA
www.redhen.org

Acknowledgments

Some of the poems in this collection first appeared in the following anthologies, journals, and magazines: "Retirement" and "Start Here" in *Chaparral*; "The Current of Desolation" and "West of the Mississippi" in *Chautauqua*; "Hibernation" in *City of the Big Shoulders: An Anthology of Chicago Poetry* (University of Iowa Press); "Forever Spinning" in *The Dos Passos Review*; "The Geographer's Wife" and "Weatherman" in *Flint Hills Review*; "Girls Like Linka" and "Raggedy Ann" in *Kokanee Review*; "Despair" in *The MacGuffin*; "Colonel Sanders (And the Gospel of Love)" and "Frame by Frame" in *Poems & Plays*; "Love is a Lumberjack with Wings" in *The Providence Journal*; "The Daily News" and "Neon Nights" in *Stone Table Review*; "The Wrong Side of Tomorrow" in *The Summerset Review*.

A debt of gratitude to Susan Cisco, Mark Cull, Kate Gale, and the entire staff at Red Hen Press. Also, thanks to the Glendale College Board of Trustees for the sabbatical granted me to complete *The Geographer's Wife*.

for Kim

Contents

EAST

NORTH

SOUTH

WEST

EAST

The Geographer's Wife

Pity the poor geographer's wife
Who spends most of her life
Missing him in every isthmus,
Desert, mountain, valley
He's had the pleasure to explore.
He claims it's not his fault—
The field takes him away,
Draws him east, west, north, and south
At a moment's notice—
Often in the middle of the night
While she rises from their tiny bed,
And he packs a bag of silence
Only a secret can keep.

He swears she knew about his desire—
The longing to touch air, land, sea—
This need to leave a piece of himself
Wherever he can, survey
The climatic conditions of an earth so vast
He can barely comprehend it all.
When she timidly asks,
Upon each of his returns,
How it is they cannot travel together—
Why he will not share his life's work—

He struggles so with his words,
She retreats to her ball of yarn
To darn yet another sock,
Steady herself for the week
They have before his next departure.

Ah, yes, pity the poor geographer's wife
Who watches the house grow
More and more around her every day.

The Contiguous 48

Before Uncle Irving died
He said he wanted to spend the night
In every state in the Union—
Or at least the contiguous 48.
He didn't seem to care
For Alaska or Hawaii,
Let alone Puerto Rico
And the other off-shore U.S. territories—
Something about a separation—
The notion that the nation
Should not suffer from marginalization,
To one degree or another.

We all thought it had to do
With Irv's own station in life,
Or lack of it, for that matter.
He always had a problem
Finding himself, more or less,
So his decision, much later in life,
To strike out on his own
In an old Ford Econoline van—
Leave us all behind—
Came as no shock or surprise.

Irv sent us a postcard each morning
When he awoke in a different state
And always claimed, should he ever return,
This is exactly where he wished "to expire"—
A term that found its way
Into much of his later correspondence.
We kept a fairly large map
On a wall in the basement
Of our home in Teaneck,
Would X out each state
With a red Magic Marker,
Where Irv last laid his tired head.

Alas though, when it came to pass,
Dear Uncle Irv eventually came up
Just a wee bit short of his goal.
He managed to hit 47 of the 48—
A phenomenal average in any sport,
Especially baseball, a game he truly loved.
Luckily, Irv was never aware of his failure.
He expired in a motel room,
Somewhere east of Rock Springs, Wyoming,
Passing his final, glorious moments in the sheets,
Peacefully asleep between two hookers from Casper

Who took his wallet, his keys,
And his van, for good measure.
Knowing Uncle Irv, he would have thought
This only right and proper,
Since he had no use whatsoever,
For any worldly goods, at this point.

Memorial Ride

Pop, you visited, once again,
In last night's dream.
I saw you washing the station wagon—
Soapy sponge in hand—
Your wavy-haired head
Nodding for me to join you,
Take the hose from your grip.
We worked together, section by section,
The way you taught me.
I listened to the song
You sang about Lulu and her baby,
But this time you actually revealed
The dirty lyrics you never sang
While Mom was still alive.
I was glad, too,
It was just the two of us—
My brothers nowhere in sight—
As we scrubbed down
The black and white Buick,
Toweled her off
Before applying the polish wax.
Then the tableau changed;
We were standing on Cedar Lane,
Watching the parade pass,

Mom right there at our side,
Mayor Feldman in his convertible,
Waving to the adoring crowd,
The VFW in their well-worn uniforms,
All the kids on their bikes,
Baseball cards clipped to their spokes,
Making the most magnificent sounds
The late May wind offered
Along this suburban route
Where time keeps steady—
Every rock ready to return—
For one more memorial ride.

Raggedy Ann

Sued her parents last week in a Manhattan courtroom
For contributing to the delinquency of a minor,
Not providing an erstwhile education,
As well as a new Chevy pickup.

Has no friends to speak of
Except that charlatan Barbie,
Who will not hang out with her again
After that drug-related incident;
Gee, can't a girl have fun?

Sits in her plush bedroom
Mumbling gibberish all day,
Trying to develop a language
Composed of nothing but vowels.

Wishes she could meet
A handsome boy called Andy
So they might form a perfect union,
Dispel the swirl of countless rumors.

Thinks she should select
Another shade of hair color,
Rather than that hideous, routine red
To brighten a rather dreary life
And rid herself of the past.

Pledges to change her meager name
To Irma, Gertrude, Bertha, or Dee—
Anything that has a taste of pizzazz!
Curse the little children who worship her;
Let them eat cake, or, better yet, mud pie.

Lights up a second pack of Camels for the day,
Deeming herself rough and ready
To trade in her striped leggings
For a black leather miniskirt
And a midnight blue beret.

Forever Spinning

This year, boys of summer
Spring into action a few weeks early
Before the competition begins.
They gather at the ballpark,
Focus on rudimentary drills—
The skills that win championships
In Pony Leagues across America.
For hours on end, by the thousands,
Players hit fungoes to each other
Until the sun sinks lower and lower
Over the municipal park diamond.

Here are the lucky kids whose parents
Do not possess the money
To send them for eight weeks to camp,
So they spend July and August
Tethered together, honing techniques
Of bat and glove, eye and speed—
This fundamental need to elevate the team
One step closer to the success
They seek before September
Drags them back to school
And the labor each textbook provides.

But here on their home field—
Littered by the refuse of time,
The grime of soiled bases,
And imaginary foul lines—
These young sons of policemen,
Bartenders, carpenters, salesmen, cooks,
Teachers, painters, librarians, plumbers,
Assemble for one more season—
A final chance to let the game survive
Inning after golden inning,
The ball forever spinning
Through the seams of their lives.

Girls Like Linka

Girls like Linka
Pin their hair to the wind—
Ten strands at a time—
When the first sign of trouble
Threatens to overtake them.

Girls like Linka
Dream of nothing but boys
Who know how to cruise
Up and down the cruel avenues
That litter their lives.

Girls like Linka
Behave badly at parties
Their mothers make them attend,
If only to raise suspicion
So they will not be invited again.

Girls like Linka
Turn away from their fathers
At that time of month,
Wishing the moon was a stranger
With a spare cigarette.

Girls like Linka
Love no one but themselves—
Always dressed in black—
Each day a service,
Every night a funeral.

The Daily News

I'm watching my weight,
Holding my tongue,
Catching my breath.

I'm hoping for love,
Waiting for fate,
Stalling for time.

I'm drawn to the chase,
Quick to the hoop,
Hip to the scene.

I'm hanging by fire,
Driving by fear,
Waking by night.

I'm playing through pain,
Jangling through June,
Soaring through space.

I'm high on speed,
Low on fuel,
Stuck on you.

GONERS

You, me and Kenny . . .
We're all dangling here
Perched high above the rapids.
One false move and we're *goners*,
As we once said in Jersey,
Long before we realized
Just how far the Passaic
Falls for each of us.
And there's no hot time
In the old town tonight,
Unless you care to count
The fire in God's belly,
Glowing ever closer, ever faster,
Lighting candle after candle
To save us from ourselves,
While we sit inside St. Anastasia's
Eating homilies for breakfast
Because tradition tells us we must.
Yet, somewhere under the apse's eye,
A devil of a shepherd lingers—
His pitchfork in hand—
Waiting for the chance
To mock this gentle flock
He leads home again.

First Kiss

She's got a great engine
And a real sweet chassis,
Cal says, stroking his new Dodge.
He's spent every penny he saved
For at least the last three years
On this tasty little truck,
Wishing I'd admire it,
Just the same as he does.
I chime in and tell him
It's really the cat's meow,
A one of a kind prize
He stole for half its worth.
But I feel like crap
'Cause what I'm staring at today,
Yesterday, and the past few months
Is his sister, Veronica.
Somehow, he's convinced her
To wash the truck with him,
And she's bending over
In these tight white shorts,
Cleaning the wheel covers—
Dark hair cascading down her back—
And it's getting to me, big time.

Not only is she his younger sister,
But she's my next door neighbor, for God's sake.
He'd murder me if he knew
The track my mind is taking.
What kind of low-life guy
Lusts after his best friend's sister?
And I'm sure I'd be able
To handle it much better
If she didn't give me
A diet of these sideways glances,
As if she somehow knows
Exactly what I'm thinking.

Wanna take her out for a spin?
Cal offers, flipping me the keys.
I gotta get ready for work,
But you're free to test her out
When Ronnie gets done hosin' her down.
Just be careful with first gear.
She sticks a bit some time.
It's all that's out of sync with her.
She just needs breakin' in.
Cal turns and walks toward the house,

Disappearing into twilight's last trance.
He doesn't see me shudder
In my ragtag leather boots.
I catch a hint of Veronica's smile,
As she peeks out at me
From below the chrome bumper.
I know my life is about to change.
I can feel it in the way
My pulse jumpstarts my heart.
And then there is nothing
But open road before us—
The taste of that first kiss.

Pretty Bird

Year after passing year
William Butler Yeats waited for the love
Maude Gonne denied him—
Smitten so that day and night
He tried writing her
Out of his life,
But it was not to be—
For her blessed vessel launched
Each line of his poetry,
Floating a fathom or two
Below the emerald sea.
Yet at some ghostly hour,
Even he must have concluded
She was everything to him
But the woman he would know
In the hollow of his bones,
Despite the words he left behind . . .
Tiny crumbs of time
A pretty bird might find
And take to the sky—
Without so much as a sigh.

TE7-6330

You could dial it now—
Just for fun, of course.
Hear who would answer
On the other end.
Explain to them, in detail,
How this was your first phone number—
Complete with the Teaneck exchange—
A lifeline, so to speak,
Your link to civilization
At such a tender age.

Here is the earliest of mantras;
Please repeat after me,
In case of emergency,
TE7-6330 . . . TE7-6330 . . . TE7-6330.
And remember to enunciate clearly;
After all, this could certainly be
A matter of life and death.

Since that time, decades ago,
You've had dozens of phone numbers
In large and small states,
Stretched across the country
To indicate your exact location—
This digital form of identification
You claim without hesitation.

But that yellow phone in the kitchen
Of the house on Warren Parkway
Never seems to disappear entirely.
And you often find, even now,
Whether you're east of Eden,
South of the border,
West of the Rockies,
Or north of the Mason-Dixon line,
When someone asks how they can reach you,
You don't hesitate to respond:
TE7-6330 . . . TE7-6330 . . . TE7-6330 . . .

Holiday

It's the first Mother's Day
You've spent without her.
You've been dreading
This day since the phone rang,
Three months ago, to let you know
How futile it all seems now—
This dumb space between thumb and mouth.

It'll be a long holiday.
You settle down with a book,
Old photographs to sort,
A cup of hot chocolate,
And Bigelow, the cat.
You've been invited out to brunch
By friends, well-meaning of course,
But somehow that doesn't seem right,
So you've decided to go it alone.

The glow of the morning sun
Provides an indelicate surprise
You hadn't bothered to anticipate—
Only the gloom May offers
This part of town you call home.
As early afternoon comes on,

You think you've got it licked
And curl up with *The New York Times:*
For news that's not fit to print.

By the hour you prepare supper—
A recipe she taught you from scratch—
You feel a bit festive
And open a bottle of wine
From a trip you both took
To the Finger Lakes, years ago,
When Mom's step was strong,
Her back steady,
Her mind sharp.

Now, as double shadows
Slowly climb the kitchen wall,
A gnawing you've never known
Takes hold and you grab the stove.
The fact that you've burned both hands
Doesn't appear to startle you;
In fact, you've been expecting it—
Like the old woman at your table
Who silently waits to be fed.

Head-On

This morning when he awoke,
He could sense the bubble
Growing halfway around her heart,
Threatening to encircle it entirely;
There was nothing he could do
To keep hope open.

It appeared, these days,
When he signaled left,
She immediately swerved right.
When he wanted in,
She was on her way out;
Meeting somewhere in the middle
Now seemed impossible.

If he knew what was wrong,
He could fix it.
He was good with automobiles:
Gears, struts, shocks, and brakes.
But women, especially this one,
Told a different story.
Without a manual in his hands,
He remained baffled.

He concluded it might be time
To cut his losses,
Hatch an escape plan,
Take the next exit off Route 80,
Drive south across the Delaware Water Gap—
Then steady the wheel before him
And pray that around the next bend
She did not meet him, head-on.

NORTH

Start Here

Start here,
In the heart of the country,
Where *Yes* is the only word
That needs to be heard—
Affirmations like candy:
A stick of sugared gum,
The sweet peppermint drop
On the tip of your tongue,
A taste the initial kiss
Left, forever, on your lips.

Start here,
In the heart of the country,
Where there is nothing
But a spare sigh
And the well-trained eye
To guide your quick step
Along the gilded path
You forgot to take,
When spring brought its offering—
One petal at a time.

Start here,
In the heart of the country,
Because nearness is so far
Across each pointed star
You swore you could reach,
In the sleepless hour
Faith drew her ring of fire
Around the halo you wore,
Long before night shadows
Whispered the answer was *No*.

WRITER'S BLOCK

My favorite student this semester tells me
She cannot write herself out of a paper bag—
A curious image, indeed.
I wonder how, for heaven's sake,
She got into the bag in the first place.
Why would she venture there?
What size is the gruesome sack?
She claims I'm missing the point.
Can't I see she has *writer's block*—
The most unfortunate of all maladies,
The nemesis of creative writing students.
I believe *harrowing* is how she describes
Her latest bout with words—
Or lack of them that offer
To pay her as much as a visit.
She says her days are surely numbered
And, I'm afraid, it's true.
For at that very moment,
A silver 6 and 7
Hang nonchalantly from her ears,
Disguising themselves as earrings.
All right, yes, I agree:

The poor girl is in a heap of trouble.
She asks me what I do
To avoid the dreaded *w.b.*
And if I am afflicted by it,
What must I do to combat
The terror when it strikes.
I think—for all of ten seconds—
Proclaim that I take a bath.
She eyes me, rather incredulously,
Demanding if it really is so.
I tell her, if nothing else,
I manage to scrub myself clean
No less than twice a week.
And if this ever fails to work,
There's always a glass of rye
Falling off a table, somewhere,
That invariably needs to be caught,
Lest it shatter upon the floor.
My student nods her head convincingly;
It's obvious she's seen whatever light
Still remains of this late winter afternoon.
She thanks me, again and again,

Before grabbing her textbooks,
Buttoning her woolen coat,
And beating it out of my office,
Preparing herself to address the snow
Now falling like miniature letters,
Sticking to the ground around her.

One Too Many Husbands

The woman with one too many husbands
Kept a secret only she possessed;
Knew the quickest way to a man's heart
Was not necessarily through his stomach—
Or through his wallet, for that matter.
No, she came to realize
All men craved a destiny
She, alone, could provide,
So she readily subscribed
To the endeavor of love,
Populating her own house—
Nine husbands at a time,
None of whom seemed to mind
Until one day it became clear
That the state's swift hand
Planned to reach out
And put an immediate stop
To what had soon become
A rather curious and profitable trade.

Though she adored each mate no less,
Even she was forced to agree
Her legal standing stood on shaky ground,

Her residence merely zoned
For eight husbands—no more.
Were it simply a measure of goats, fowl, or equine,
Everything might have been quickly resolved,
But this certainly was not the case,
And she feared a spate of lawsuits,
Undermining her life's work.
Therefore, over the course of many years,
She always had an extra husband about,
Who had to be shipped out
To Duluth, Lincoln, or Sioux City—
Places where their faces were never lost,
Just rotated for a while—
Circulated, so that she could keep
The wheel of love in motion—
This steady, eternal devotion
To spouse after spouse after spouse.

HIBERNATION

You have to think it's simply
A matter of hibernation—
Perhaps, the longest on record,
But nothing more than that.
The odds must slowly
Slide in our favor—
Over 100 seasons waiting
For just the right year
To end this drought,
Throw back our big shoulders.

The best and the brightest
Ever to play the game
Came here to the Friendly Confines
To wave the hickory stick,
Pitch fastballs of fire,
Unleash the bleachers' desire
For that last bottle of Bud,
Prior to Harry's sweet call
To take us out to the ball game.

Who really knows?
Maybe it was the curse of the goat
Or too much illumination,
Instead of the natural light that arrives
Before the end of sleep
And the eternal promise
October offers this windy city,
In exchange for another home run
Flying high above the ivy-filled wall
With no return in sight.

Surely, Ernie would still love to play two
If given half the chance
To tinker forever in a Cubbies uniform.
Billy, Fergie, Gabby, Kenny, Ron, and Ryne
Only need to wake from slumber's embrace
And set the record straight—
Run the table, wire to wire,
As if 1908 were yesterday
And we could hear
The bear roar once more.

The New Math

Fuzzy at best,
Something I must attempt
If ever I can find the time
To sit down and forget
What it is I thought I knew.
Take you and me, for instance.
We ought to calculate
The pluses and minuses
Before we go any further,
Yet that doesn't seem
To stop us from barreling
Headlong into the wind—
If you subtract a lull or two.
I mean, the trouble we faced
The year before last,
Concerning the division of labor
Under this roof we share,
Certainly is a thing of the past;
Wouldn't you agree?
Thank goodness, we no longer discuss
The silly need you have to multiply,
Adding new mouths by the moment;
Who would be able to total it all?
It appears I'm quite comfortable

With the systematic treatment
Our relationship affords us—
This magnitude of figure and form
I number in the space
I have reserved for you—
A simple problem to solve.

SNOUTS

Snout of the sky,
Snout of the sun,
Snout of the work
Until it is done.

Snout of the dog,
Snout of the pig,
Snout of the small
Until it is big.

Snout of the girl,
Snout of the boy,
Snout of the grief
Until it is joy.

Snout of the nun,
Snout of the priest,
Snout of the wheat
Until it is yeast.

Snout of the soul,
Snout of the heart,
Snout of the light
Until it is dark.

Snout of the moon,
Snout of the stars,
Goodnight my sweet snouts
Wherever you are.

The Church of Dislocation

You've given serious thought
To Joplin or Joliet,
Davenport or Deadwood;
You'd like to move someplace
Where no one knows your business—
Least of all your name.
You've committed no crime
For or against society,
Certainly none you can recall;
There's no warrant for your arrest—
In any state of the union—
And palimony, matrimony and alimony
Do not concern you for the moment.
Face it, my friend;
You're one free dude.

In less than an hour
You could pack a suitcase,
Discard the junk in your apartment,
Leave this cow town behind;
Who really would be the wiser?
You have no timeline,
Not a single cloud on the horizon,
And your next destination

Waits like a coming attraction
On the thin windshield before you.
Other guys would easily die
For this geographical liberation—
An introduction to your new religion:
The Church of Dislocation.

Soon, you'll be ready to hit the road;
It won't be long before you'll praise
The blur in the rear-view mirror
As you blow past the last goodbye.

Romantic Bones

Every now and then
She throws these romantic bones,
Makes me grovel at her feet,
Does what she can
To keep me on her leash.

I'm a bit of a hound dog,
Moping my nights away . . .
But I do love a good read.
Time and time again
I fetch my favorite book,
The Fine Art of Retreat,
Yet, somehow, I never manage
To turn even a single page—
What with these cumbersome paws
Growing larger and larger each day.

I have half a mind
To take a walk one morning
With her at my side,
Just simply bolt—
Turn tail, as they say,
Make my way to freedom I deserve,
Instead of the link and chain,

Strangling my neck and brain,
Until I'm unable to stand up straight.

But no, here I stay,
Loyal to her I remain,
Although it may be the death of me.
Ah yes, now comes the sweet kiss,
A back rub before din-din,
The gentle stroke under my chin,
And there it is—finally—
The prize in her delicate hand,
This ultimate reward I demand,
A token I bury in a backyard plot,
Six feet above my pride.

SEVEN

A week's worth of work—
That's how they described them—
Seven to be exact,
One for each day, of course;
What reason was there for more?

Monday, the first of the lot,
Had auburn hair and curls.
Her eyes brooded, non-stop,
But she was good with the others
And wore her burden well.

Tuesday cursed her big sister,
Watched her blond, limp tresses
Hang straight as a rope.
She studied the black arts
And cast spells in the dark.

Wednesday was a happy sort
Who gave herself over to God.
She learned, quite early,
How easily grace became her,
Sharing whatever she could with the poor.

Thursday defied all the odds,
Just surviving as she did—
Not much bigger than a minute—
But she climbed the corporate ladder
And ate her rivals for breakfast.

Friday had no head for work;
She communed with nature
And dabbled in the written word.
When the forest called her,
She did her best to listen.

Saturday was blinded by fate,
Cursing the alcohol she sought to escape.
The lure of the street intoxicated her—
Well beyond the legal limit—
No home could contain her.

Sunday never left her parents' side,
Taking care of their needs,
Until the moment they died.
A quiet girl, content to keep the peace,
She lived to be a hundred and three.

DESPAIR

I am done with despair—
Decided to cross it off
The extensive list of things
I need to accomplish today.
I have lived too long
In the center of its grip,
Always hoping my tall shadow
Would save the small part of me
I deemed worthy of salvation.
Now I turn away its yoke,
Even joke about the black dog—
And its habitual bark—
Who once chased me down
Desolation's dark alley—
Two short blocks from the house
I built, brick by brick.
Let another poor soul wallow,
Like a lovesick calf,
Night after captive night—
Merely for the sake of it;
Perhaps, it will do him good.
But I have a plane to catch,
A train to board,
A ship to sail,

As I patiently await
The hour of embarkation—
My left leg steady as a rail,
My right hand, open and ready,
To welcome aboard the next passenger.

The Almighty Plate

Lately, she can not stop
Consuming everything in sight:
Morning, noon, and night.
She falls asleep, ravenous,
And dreams of banquets—
Tables laden with meats,
Delicious treats to devour,
Hour after hour.

For each vision she proffers,
There is no meal
She is unable to finish
During a single sitting.
Now that she worships
At the altar of The Almighty Plate,
She is always well equipped
With her silver fork and golden knife—
Best friends in this new life.

Her family has sought counsel
From the clergy and its flock,
As well as the medical trade,
But, sadly, to no avail.
Even the intervention they planned,

Failed miserably when she simply
Locked the doors to her house,
Shut all the relatives out,
And ate her way into the next day.

Still, they pray for an awakening—
Some miracle of sorts to turn her
Inside out, upside down,
So tired are they of spying—
Through the kitchen window—
The utterly round woman
Who continues to grow
At such an alarming rate,
No one can predict her fate.

PRAIRIE DANCE

Helicopters don't normally fall from the sky,
Plummet to earth in a heap,
But this one did—
Directly above Platte County,
Grand Prairie, Nebraska,
253 Darewood Lane, to be exact.

Killed were veteran pilot Mal Adams,
Passengers Carey Dwayne Clark,
His wife, Stacy Rae,
Their infant daughter, Claire.
The one hour pleasure ride
Billed itself as a unique opportunity
To see the rolling hills from a bird's eye view.
The Clarks took the trip to celebrate
Ten years of wedded bliss.

The wayward craft also flattened the house
Belonging to Kip Rogers, Jr.
And his wife, Wilma,
Who were dead on arrival
At Mercy Memorial Hospital,
Along with their twin boys, Clark and Earl.

That the accident only damaged
A single house on the block,
Caused Chief of Police Vern Suggs
And Fire Captain Lee Armstrong
To exclaim surely a miracle
Occurred that August afternoon in 2002
At 3:12 p.m., Central Standard Time.

The NTSB arrived the next morning,
Dispatching an expert team to determine
The cause of the fiery accident—
The reason for life and property loss;
However, one year later,
They were still unsure
What brought the spinning machine
So quickly down to the ground.

Pilot error?
Mechanical failure?
Poor visibility and other related trouble?
Perhaps, all of the above,
Maybe none of it, whatsoever,
Played a fatal role
In this chance prairie dance—
One sunny summer afternoon.

Seamstresses

It tears at the fabric—
Ritual love we repair—
So seamless in its pattern,
So fickle in its spite.
We work through silence,
One thimble at a time,
Guile's long golden needles
Pointing straight towards the sky.
I thread, you mend;
You loop, I rend.
We no longer pretend
We know what reparations are due.
And yet we stitch on,
One season after another,
Each new design a landscape
Unfettered by useless measure—
This simple act of desire
We weave into the clothes we wear.

SOUTH

Colonel Sanders (And the Gospel of Love)

Colonel Sanders speaks of love,
But, alas, no one will listen.
He's close to 120 years old,
Knows he may ultimately be knocking
On the door to chicken fried heaven;
Therefore, he needs to preach
And reach each available ear,
This side east of the Mississippi.
The Good Lord saved him thirty years ago—
Delivered his God-fearing soul
From acute leukemia and pneumonia
In December of 1980—
Allowed his spirit to be reborn,
Spread salvation's sweet secret
To man, woman, and child;
However, they all appear deaf,
Unable to hear word one.

Every evening, approaching midnight,
Harlan visits a different franchise,
Lays his wrinkled, veined hands
Over the breast, legs, thighs, and wings
Of the poultry he believes
Will carry hope's eternal message

Through the sacred channels of digestion.
He massages the dear severed birds
Long into the early morning hours,
Before he leaves to tackle the day's toil,
Witnessing on street corners in the New South—
Unrecognizable without the white suit,
Mustache and goatee he gave up three decades ago
When he discovered light so divine,
He need not dress for dinner again.
Yet there's much work ahead . . .
The Colonel prays, in his final days,
To find the strength to continue revealing
How the power of goodness and grace
Always fills up the empty space
Between God, chicken, and man.

South of the Border

She tells me she should go
South of the border—
A place where order
Will no longer dictate
The life she must lead.

She throws her espresso hair
Across her narrow shoulders,
Packs the canvas bag
That always remains open
By the foot of her bed.

It has come to this—
As I knew it would.
For the first time
I find the meter
In my head silent:
The absence of tick or tock—
Click or clock.

She can not live another day
Under the thumb I press
To keep her in line, she says.
I ask where she will go,

What she will do,
Who does she know in Rio Bravo?
But to her it is of no matter;
Neither truth, nor consequence.

I question her about money
And she merely laughs.
She will live off the land—
Demand only of herself
What she is able to give . . .
Control the means of her own production.

Soon, there is nothing more
Than the sound her steps make,
Striking the stairs in the steady beat
The rain drops above my head,
As I sleep during a summer shower.

The quiet house summons me
To capture each spare moment.
I light a cigar in the dark,

Blow smoke rings towards the ceiling—
Wonder how long it will take
Before her arms grow weary,
Her spine unsteady,
Her feet ready for comfortable shoes.

Tombstone Territory

In the late model automobile
We sit by the side of the road,
Drunk again on lost words
We keep waiting to hear,
Like the slow sound bourbon makes
As it snakes into the tall glass
You pour yourself each evening
After a hard day at work.

I could say this was not
What I bargained for, years ago,
But I am as much to blame
As the haze of alcohol
You lately desire, more than me.
I have heard of women
Who have driven men to drink,
But this, I suppose,
Is just wishful thinking,
When I know, full well,
We suffer least who suffer what we choose,
And the demon booze you imbibe
May merely be God in disguise,
Setting us straight with a straw.

Yet I am not ready
To quit whatever safety
I find behind fate's door,
Enduring my long wait,
Huddled here in the rear seat of our car,
Whose motor has simply decided
Not to turn over this time,
Leaving us in tombstone territory—
One grave away from home.

THE CURRENT OF DESOLATION

The current of desolation
Runs east to west, north to south,
But that certainly does not cover it all.
Who will eventually speak up
For the sorrow of the Sacramento,
The howl of the Hudson,
The grief of the Great Lakes,
The misery of the Mississippi.
Season after season,
We water the arid land—
Wherever it is we can—
From one coast to the other,
These tributaries of tears,
Flowing in either direction,
And then slowly back again.
How else do we dictate
What trails our misfortunes take,
In the wake of each break,
Struggling to reach a recalcitrant shore.
Perhaps, one day soon,
We will all live beneath the sea—
Melancholy but free—
Happy, at last,
Never to open the sky.

Love is a Lumberjack with Wings

Love is a lumberjack with wings,
Flying so high above your head
You fail to notice anything
Out of the ordinary,
Until it's too late
And the saw softly falls
Squarely between your shoulders—
So much for *Have a nice day.*

Love is an acrobat on speed,
Unconcerned about a misstep here
Or a mishap there;
What's a limber body for, anyway?
Why not alter the routine
You practice on the balance beam?
And should you break a leg—
Take two and call me in the morning.

Love is a banker in denial,
Never willing to smile
At the almighty dollar sign
Flashing before his eyes,
Or the Traveler's Checks
He swears he can do without
When he enters no man's land—
Unaware of the legal tender.

This Time of Year

This time of year
Everything drifts south;
It all goes somewhere downwind,
Below the night's regal shadow,
Under a cradle we rock.
We've long grown familiar
With this curious course of life—
A direction that overtakes us
No matter what we do.
It all appears to fall
Ingloriously through our hands:
Barrettes, casseroles, coins, remote controls—
Whatever it is we touch.
And then there are the intangibles
We drop during the day:
Compliments, curses, invitations, promises.
But it's the sheer act of tumbling
We never quite seem to grasp—
This constant head over heels motion,
Being parallel to the pavement,
When every single bone
(We don't want to break)
Tells us we should remain perpendicular,

Upright, masters of our fate.
Thank goodness, we all suffer together,
Know what to expect each season
The tumult comes calling,
Like an old, trusted friend
We refuse to turn away.

The Gravity of Silence

He hands you a quarter,
Tells you to phone your mother,
Suggests she can pick you up,
Sometime, later that night,
And parent you all over again,
So you don't cling to him
Like the tight pants around his waist.
He's had it with you,
Says he's through;
He can't take it any longer
And would rather live alone
Than share the box you call home.

You've been waiting for this for weeks,
Knowing the end was near,
Fearing the sound his boot would make
The final time it hit the ground;
It's clear how this drama plays out.
You can hear him in the bedroom,
Opening up closets and drawers,
Tossing clothes into the suitcase
You bought him last Christmas
When you both moved to Lake Charles
For the job he'd been promised,

Working for the Lucky Star Casino,
But the downturn in the economy
Soon did away with that.

Maybe Mama would take you back.
It's been well over a year
Since Daddy succumbed to his heart attack.
Your only sister left Lafayette
To form corporate mergers outside of Houston;
You could stay in her room for a while.
But now he's in the kitchen,
Gathering an object or two.
He claims he'll return tomorrow
For the rest of his possessions,
Barely glancing at you as he speaks.
Then he's out the door—
Heavy steps on the landing—
Before you're suddenly struck
By the gravity of silence . . .
A world without him.

Retirement

Sat on the shelf
In a curious corner
Of an odd room
I left long ago—
When I didn't presume
I'd ever need claim it
But could just as easily
Allow it to rest
In the remote place
I thought was shelter.

Who could approach it then?
When the dreaded sound
Of the tick tock in its belly
Wound down each day,
As if the next hour doomed
The enormous clock I wore
Strapped to my chest
For the world to see.

Now I find I envy
The life of a hobo,
Whose toes keep him

Forever on the go—
Following only the row
Of track after track,
A straight line set
Against the distant horizon
And the stink eye of time.

Topographical Error

It wasn't where she wanted to be—
Not how the dream should surface.
There were no mountains or oceans
To make her feel complete;
Even the sun, when it did shine,
Left a dusky haze in its wake,
Taking a tiny piece of her each day
Before twilight routinely split
What was left of her in half.

She never would have settled here,
In the Panhandle, of all places,
Had it not been for him.
Him, him, him, him!
It was always him—
Those big ideas of his,
Leaving the coast for open spaces
He claimed would do them wonders,
Make them stewards of the land
No man could replicate.

Now there is the baby . . .
His choice, of course,
Bouncing around in her belly—

This lucky caged animal,
Ready to escape in two months
When the earth will refuse to spin,
Trapping her forever—
Without topography or weather—
Precious lifeline gone.

Perhaps, on the baby's fifth birthday,
Prior to its kindergarten enrollment,
She could attempt to convince him
That for the child's sake,
A move home would be sensible.
If not, she had already begun
To hide mad money,
Like the red squirrels she spied every fall,
Blanketing the flat plains before her.

Lost Dog

PLEASE HELP US!
SIZEABLE REWARD OFFERED!
(No questions asked)
For the safe return of *Bruno*,
A down and out German Shepherd
Who answers to *Betsy*,
Last seen in Jefferson Parish,
Approximately 10 a.m. Friday morning,
Wearing absolutely nothing—
Naked, nude, without shame.

Dog could be headed west
On his way out of town,
Or south, just to see the sights.
He, or she, as the case may be,
Occasionally limps, mainly for sympathy.
Sports a tattoo of Rin Tin Tin
Impeccably inked on hindquarters,
And may very well whimper
At the sight of a T-bone steak.

Loving and trusted family member,
Devoted to digging up the garden,
Simply for the sheer joy of it,

Gnawing through a succession of couches,
Flunking out of countless obedience schools,
And stealing the neighbors' newspapers—
But only on Sunday.
Our children remain bereft—
Grief etched on their tiny faces.
They keep asking, again and again,
When *Susie* will come home.

The situation appears bleak.
After all, it's been more
Than a few years now.
Anyone, anywhere, at any time,
Please feel free to rescue us;
Don't hesitate to phone—
No matter the hour,
Should you spy *Charlie*
Peeing by the side of the highway.
We miss the poor little whelp
More than words convey.

Decisions

We have decided to move;
Pick up stakes, as they say,
Light out for territory unknown,
View landscape so different
We can't quite imagine
Where our feet will touch ground.

We have decided to sell:
House, car, camera, cat—
The children, if need be—
Everything to cut us free,
Leave the familiar behind,
Climb into obscurity.

We have decided to depart—
The night after tomorrow—
Just when the moon splinters
And no soul witnesses our escape,
Except for a shadow's trace
Lingering by the kitchen door.

We have decided to reveal
Not even the hint of a plan
To God above or the devil below;

Just grant us good speed
And a generous breeze,
Placing us upon the path.

We have decided to exchange
One last gasp at the past,
Before our next vow
Teaches how patiently faith
Allows us to travel
This open road together.

The Wrong Side of Tomorrow

Each morning we wake up
On the wrong side of tomorrow—
Fresh tracks from the evening
Running down the length of our backs.
We say today will be different;
We adjust our engineer's caps,
Climb aboard the locomotive
We've ridden through life—
This long train of spite
We drive deep into night.
We try to obey the traffic signs
Standing between our destinations,
But there are far too many
To yield the right of way—
One cautionary tale after the other,
As far as the eye can see.
And, still, this never-ending line
Provides the only comfort we know:
The hum of each rail beneath us,
The glow of the engine's fire,
The steady tick of the brakeman's watch—
As if we could safely measure the future,
By the time it takes to arrive.

The Deep South

It's when she's traveling
Down to the Deep South,
And the lights are out
In the rooms of our little house
That she softly asks
If our love is enough
To leave me grounded—
Steady on the rock
She keeps ready in her pocket,
Should I ever need it.
I stroke her tired head,
Hoping to send her off
To the sleep she deserves,
Where there are no questions,
Only silent answers in the dark
We choose to share together—
One benevolent night at a time.
Here we learn to abandon
A kaleidoscope of dreams,
Trading desire back and forth
To witness the next sunrise
And know how much it is ours.
At rest, in the chance moments

The early morning allows,
We lie in the empty space
Our simple embrace provides—
The hint of another vow,
Gently clinging to our skin.

WEST

FRAME BY FRAME

You're Laura Linney,
Trapped in a phone booth,
Calico cat on your head.

I'm Joe Biden,
Flubbing one more joke
By the side of the campaign trail.

We're a comical pair,
Preparing to meet our Maker
Where X marks the spot.

I sense the camera's angle,
A boom dangles overhead;
How many T's are there in trouble?

You watch this futile dance,
Popcorned to the screen,
Dirty martini in hand.

We turn down the sound,
Crawl into our Hollywood bed,
Relight what's left of the night.

WEST OF THE MISSISSIPPI

These days we're always
West of the Mississippi,
One state away from tomorrow—
The only remaining small town—
Unidentifiable on a stranger's map.
We've packed our bags so many times
It now appears useless
To have any destination in mind;
Better to drift towards eternity
With nothing but itinerant wind.

Often, we allow the river
To dictate our slow progress,
Skirting the steep sweep of banks
That swell when the water
Crests up to meet them,
Testing tide after tide,
Dropping the curious leadline
The dead leave behind.

No longer do we find our fate
In the promise of the frontier,
Far too late to investigate
Anything further than the taut truth,

Whose limitless boundaries border
These simple steps we take,
Making a life for ourselves—
The bifurcation of all we know:
Come north, south, east, west.

Breakdown

F. Scott Fitzgerald slowly surfaces
From a long night of boozing—
Another quarrel with Zelda
That makes the neighbors
Close their bedroom windows
On this sweltering summer night.
Scott hates to see his wife out of control,
Always thinks her return from the hospital
Will be the dawn of a new day,
The *miracle* as he prefers to say.
But she is overwrought again,
Claiming he cares not a wit
For her and her own work—
Save, perhaps, her paintings—
Which threaten him less than her writing.
Scott figures he'll wait this waltz out,
The same dance they rehearse,
As if they're auditioning for a play
Whose roles have already been cast.
Zelda keeps repeating the word,
Grim, grim, grim, under her breath,
Scott thinking it must be the name
Of another lover she's taken,

Even in her petrified, fragile state.
Then, as if nothing whatsoever occurred,
There is the cargo of kisses,
Tomorrow's sweet promises,
The praise and hope for Scottie's
First year of boarding school—
This couple who cheerfully prepare
For the next capricious round
In the shadow of one more breakdown.

WEATHERMAN

I'm trying to read the weather—
Render a perfect forecast—
Predict where and when
The Santa Anas will blow next—
Wonder what has become of El Niño . . .
If he plans to return—
Fist full of a young boy's fury.

I'm obsessed with sun and rain,
Hot and cold, mist and frost.
I've given up my job at the plant,
Divorced my wife and dog,
Spent my last dollar on nothing
Short of the sublime squalor
My life has now become.

I don't need a meteorologist
On the 11 o'clock news—
Dressed in a fancy suit—
To tell me which way the wind blows
Or how the clouds are massing up
Above the San Gabriel Mountains.
I have my own barometer
And intend to employ it

For purposes that only God and I
May choose to divulge in the future.

Heavens above, earthquakes below;
One day I'll know how to pinpoint
What nature has in store for me—
This climatic gyration I face each day,
Without rhyme or reason,
Season after season,
Leaving me to ponder
Whether the threat of weather
Keeps me indoors, forever.

Sex Me

I want you to sex me.
She was a 19-year-old student
Who had recently taken my final exam
At the university where I taught.
There was a wild party
Inside the faculty club in Ibadan,
The week before I returned to Los Angeles.
We were all dancing the highlife—
Expatriates everywhere in sight.
The evening soon would be morning,
But her glistening skin always remained
The rich color of night.

I want you to sex me.
We stood on a balcony,
Surrounded by palm fronds,
Trying to escape the summer heat,
While the music's rapid beat
Enveloped us in a tight fist.
She was the daughter of a diplomat—
This much I certainly knew.
When she called me by my first name,
I heard the sky crack
And the wind moan;
I told her she should be going home.

I want you to sex me.
She took hold of my hand
And placed it upon her hip,
Drawing me further into the circle
She formed for the two of us.
I did not refuse the meeting
Until a very burly man came
To hustle the poor girl away.
He told me I was in danger
And left me with nothing more
Than her shadow's afterglow.

Neon Nights

You think you've fashioned a life
Out of the chaos of hope—
Taken enough to make amends
For the shortcomings that keep you up,
Long into another neon night.
It's nothing but a crapshoot,
Even though you toss the dice
Against the curb of desire,
Watching each cube tumble and spin,
Knowing you have as much chance to win
As the whore with twelve locks on her door.

What were the odds you would go straight
When you followed the dangerous road
Down Dead Man's Curve,
Then back again,
Sometimes, twice in the same light.
Why didn't you suspect the moon
Had a knife in her fat purse,
And she wasn't afraid to use it
Before her tired hand fell asleep.
Better to be alert and ready
Than unsteady on your feet.

The next time you take a trip
Be sure to unpack your lies
So you won't feel far from home.
Dress appropriately for inclement weather,
Never remove the hat on your head,
Employ an alias to disguise appearances,
Reverse the normal smile
You reserve to meet the public.
But privately speaking, of course,
You're still afraid of the dark.

Out of My Life

I could write you out of my life;
Surely, it wouldn't take much time.
I could alter our history—
A day here, a few nights there—
Condemn us to a past
Where paths never crossed . . .
Not for one measly minute.

We could make a go of it—
Separately, of course;
You on your coast,
Me on the other,
Paddling our way to what?
Solitary happiness, at best?
Perhaps, wolfishness, at least?

Who can possibly chart
The course our lives travel,
Buried on pages, confined to stanzas,
Linked lines with single words,
Spelled out letter by letter—
Until our ancient alphabet
Loses its propensity for love.

But all that being said . . .
I'm loath to advance the next step—
Change what we've become—
Temper our initial meeting's tale;
Mere chance—or act of God?
When the matter before us is simply
Your tongue, my lips,
My glance, your kiss—
This one attempt at bliss
We are unable to resist.

I Read My Mother to Sleep

Almost three years
Removed from my mother's death,
I study the list of books
She sent at my request,
Six months earlier,
When she was still able to write
And her mind remained open,
Free of the disease whose claim
She could not escape.

Mother laughed when I asked
For her personal recommendations—
Avid reader that she was—
And told me in short order
She would jot down her favorites.
Somehow, she seemed surprised
I would value what books
Impacted the long life she led—
Made her the woman I admired.

Now, lucky man that I am,
With the pasture of time
Freshly spread before me,
And this semester's sabbatical

A sure thing, even in an awkward age,
I turn the page containing
The secret works my mother chose—
Those that surely sustained her
In her hour of need.

How curious then is my find:
Here's Trollope, Williams, and Graham,
Hegi, Mitchard, and Haley—
Authors who transport me
From the end of an ocean
To small stones from a river.
Tonight, let the journey begin . . .
I read my mother to sleep.

Under Construction

There's a break in the weather
So the crew can work today.
It's been raining all week.
I'm pretty well dismayed;
The job will take far longer
Than we first anticipated.
I also slowly realize
This means more money in their pockets—
Much less in mine—
The price tag of major construction
During the early spring season,
Here, in sunny California.

We haven't even begun
The planting stage yet—
Too busy with the hardscape,
One retaining wall after another—
This concrete city springing up
Around my little house
To stop the hillside from spilling down,
Swallowing me like an enormous fish,
Too famished for its own good.
Then there's the matter of the patio—
Slate, tile, or brick, if you prefer,
Not to mention cobblestone.

I keep thinking there aren't enough plans drawn—
That the architect's dropped the ball
Somewhere between here and Altadena,
And I ought to go to Gus's
With Armando, the foreman,
Who'll steady my nerves at the bar,
Since he'll tell me it's all running smoothly . . .
Everything is fully under control,
Block by block by block.
It's just unsettling each night—
Climbing into bed without the woman
You swore was your wife.

Takin' Stock

331 LPs (Bach to Beatles to Blues to Broadway)
220 novels (for the hero, highbrow, and the popular mind)
117 bottles of wine (red, of course—okay, one bottle of chardonnay)
84 CDs (keep movin' folks . . . nothing to see here)
53 freshmen and sophomore students (light semester, indeed!)
40 outdoor path and spotlights (you can't see in the dark, can you?)
34 sport jackets (good lord, keep 'em comin')
29 pairs of boots (and that's the truth)
17 doors (various heights, lengths, widths, styles)
14 pairs of jeans (some frayed, some new—all 34x34)
13 steep steps (to lift you up to the loft)
11 wooden slat beech blinds (to keep the riffraff out)
8 cowboy hats (surely you've heard of Black Bart)
7 neighbors (that's what you get for living at the base of a hillside)
5 telephones (two corded, two cordless, and one cell)
4 plum trees (along the backyard fence—just for show)
3 bathrooms (his, hers, possibly yours???)
2 televisions (old style—sorry, no plasma, HD, or large screen)
1 1998 Toyota 4-Runner (94,275 miles—excellent condition)
No mortgage, no pets, no children, no mate.

Go, Prepare, Surrender

Tomorrow, at dawn, you'll awake
To the gift by your side—
The one you've awaited, it seems,
Almost all your life.
It will not arrive in the mail;
It will not knock upon your door.
It will, however, enter unannounced,
Expecting nothing in return
For the service it provides.

Day by day, you'll discover
A certain sense of wonder
As it makes itself at home,
Measuring the space between you
And the rest of the world.
Soon, you'll divine light
From the curious shadow thrown
Halfway across each room—
Morning, noon, and night.

In due time, you may grow
So familiar with its presence
You might think it's disappeared,

But you'll always know it's there—
This steady ring of promise
You swore you'd never wear.
Yet, simply for now:
Go, prepare, surrender
To the future before you . . .

The Happiest Man Alive
for Henry Miller

I've got my back to the wall—
Cash poor and out of scratch.
There's shit on my shoes,
My dog has disowned me
And placed an ad for a new master
In today's edition of *The Daily Growl*,
Barking up a storm
With all the other bitches
From the neighborhood pound.

I have nowhere to live;
Being between a rock and a hard place
Suddenly seems appealing to me.
I'm down on my luck
Because I don't know which end is up
And that makes me nauseous, to boot.

There's a growth on my neck—
The size of Saskatchewan.
The only doctor I know
Refuses to see me since I fondled
A rubber female model
While waiting for him in his office.

My sister repeatedly claims
I have bats in the belfry,
But the last time I checked,
My church refused to allow me in;
Nothing flew above my head,
Save an occasional baseball or two.

Let's face it; I have neither prospects,
Nor the wherewithal for success
In this labor intensive domain,
And, yet, whistling to myself—
Decidedly off-key in the rain—
I'm the happiest man alive.

LATITUDE/LONGITUDE

Latitude – 34.136835 N
Longitude – 118.18267 W
A measure by no other means,
Just as simple as that,
This basic life neatly coordinated
One tiny degree at a time;
Elliptical lines of angular distance:
East and west from the meridian,
North and south from the equator—
A public sense of identity
Privacy can never hide.

Yes, that's exactly where I am.
Here you'll find me night and day,
One season following another,
Week by patient week;
After all, don't they always say:
Location, location, location?
There's no reason to wander—
Certainly no purpose to explore
Any territory other than mine.

I can work countless geographic equations
Until I'm blue in the face,
Calculate the space between nautical miles,
Give or take a pole or two,
But, honestly, why even bother?
When I know no other perfect number
Than the one I'm assigned—
This earthly promise that aligns me
To sun, moon, star and sky.

Photo credit: Greg Parks

Biographical Note

Bart Edelman was born in Paterson, New Jersey, in 1951, and spent his childhood in Teaneck. He received his undergraduate and graduate degrees from Hofstra University. He is currently professor of English at Glendale College, where he edits *Eclipse*, a literary journal. He has been awarded grants and fellowships from the United States Department of Education, the University of Southern California, and the L.B.J. School of Public Affairs at the University of Texas at Austin, and conducted literary research in India, Egypt, Nigeria and Poland. His poetry has appeared in newspapers, journals, textbooks and anthologies, published by City Lights Books, Etruscan Press, Harcourt Brace, McGraw-Hill, Prentice Hall, Simon & Schuster, Thomson/Heinle and the University of Iowa Press. He teaches poetry workshops across the United States and was Poet-in-Residence at Monroe College of the State University of New York. Collections of his work include *Crossing the Hackensack* (1993), *Under Damaris' Dress* (1996), *The Alphabet of Love* (1999), *The Gentle Man* (2001), and *The Last Mojito* (2005). He lives in Pasadena, California.